dabble lab

ELECTRONICS
PROJECTS TO BUILD ON
4D An Augmented Reading Experience

BY TAMMY ENZ

CONSULTANT: TOM HONZ

Teacher Librarian/Media Specialist
Centennial High School
Ankeny, Iowa

CAPSTONE PRESS
a capstone imprint

Dabble Lab is published by Capstone Press,
1710 Roe Crest Drive, North Mankato, Minnesota 56003
www.mycapstone.com

Library of Congress Cataloging-in-Publication Data
ISBN 978-1-5435-2846-6 (library binding)
ISBN 978-1-5435-2850-3 (paperback)
ISBN 978-1-5435-2854-1 (eBook PDF)

Editorial Credits:
Mari Bolte, editor; Heidi Thompson, designer; Morgan Walters, media researcher;
Laura Manthe, production specialist

Photo Credits:
All images by Capstone Studio, Karon Dubke
Shutterstock: 4 Girls 1 Boy, (grid) design element throughout, sirtravelalot, 5,
VectorPot (gears) design element throughout

Printed in the United States of America.
PA49

TABLE OF CONTENTS

LIGHT IT UP

Electronics power our world. From the lights that help us see to the satellites that allow us to communicate across the globe, we rely on electricity all day, every day.

Learn the science behind little lights, brilliant breadboards, and short circuits. You may be starting out small, but someday you could light up the world.

1. Ask an adult to download the app.  Capstone 4D Education

2. Scan any page with the star.

3. Enjoy your cool stuff!

————— OR —————

Use this password at capstone4D.com

nextlevel.electronics

⭐ USING LEDS

Light-emitting diode (LED) lights are small but powerful. When paired with a power source, these little bulbs light up and let you know your electrical experiment is on the right track.

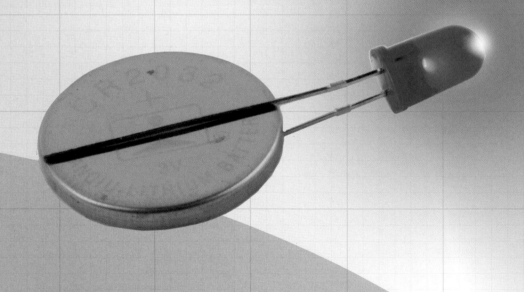

 FACT LEDs glow when electrical current passes through them. The longer lead on an LED is positive '+'. It must be connected to the positive '+' side of the battery.

LIGHTS ON

Wiring up the lights in a house seems like a big job. Many electrical circuits run through walls to get switches and lights to work. But you can make your own simple circuit in a snap.

YOU'LL NEED

> CR2032 battery
> 5mm LED
> electrical tape

STEPS

1 Slide the battery between the leads of the LED. Make sure the longer lead is touching the '+' side of the battery. The shorter lead should touch the '-' side of the battery.

2 Wrap the tape around the battery to hold the LED in place.

3 To turn the LED off, unwrap the tape and remove the LED.

 FACT The power source for this project is a battery. A different type of power lights up the bulbs in your home. NEVER experiment with the outlets in your home. That power source is very strong and can be dangerous.

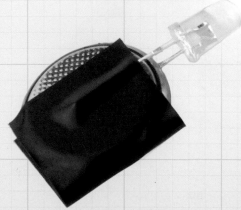

FIREWORKS FLINGER

Use your LEDs to light up the night sky. Give your circuit a super simple switch and then send it spinning.

YOU'LL NEED

> CR2032 battery

> 5mm LED

> hot glue and hot glue gun

> three 0.25-by-6-inch (0.6-by-15.2-cm) strips of cellophane

> sturdy index card

STEPS

1 Slide the battery between the LED leads.

2 Make sure the longer lead is touching the '+' side of the battery. The shorter lead should touch the '-' side of the battery.

3 Glue the '+' lead to the '+' side of the battery.

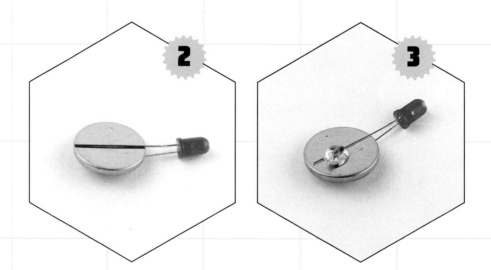

 FACT LEDs come in many different colors. The materials contained inside them makes their color. Make your fireworks show in a rainbow of colors. How many can you send off at once?

4   Glue the cellophane strips to the '+' side of the battery.

5   Fold the index card in half the long way.

6   Slide the folded card under the '-' lead. The LED should turn off.

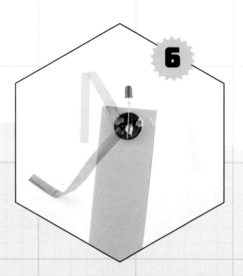

7   Hold the other end of the card. Then give it a flick to send the battery flying.

FACT A circuit is a complete and closed path that allows electrical current to flow. In this case, it flows from one side of a battery through an LED. Then it flows back to the other side of the battery. When the circuit is opened, the flow of electricity is broken. The card's presence prevents this flow of electricity. The LED will stop glowing until the card is removed. The card acts like a simple switch.

ALL ABOUT CIRCUITS

Sometimes the light or gadget you need to power is far from the power source. If so, you need to create a way to get the electricity where you need it. Copper tape is the key.

SIMPLE CIRCUIT

Let the electricity flow! Start with a simple circuit to send electricity from your power source straight to an LED.

YOU'LL NEED

> two 6-inch- (15-cm-) long pieces of conductive copper tape

> CR2032 battery

> 5mm LED

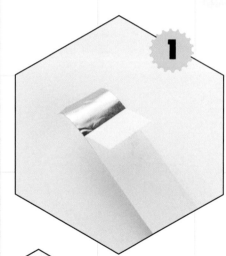

STEPS

1. Peel a ½-inch (1.3-cm) section of backing from each end of one copper tape strip.

2. Stick one end of the tape to the '+' side of the battery.

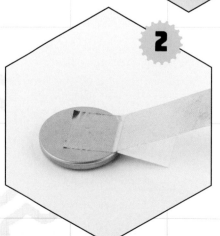

3   Wrap the other end of the tape around the LED's longer lead.

4   Repeat step 1 with the second piece of tape.

5   Stick one end of the tape to the '-' side of the battery. Make sure the pieces of copper angle away from one another slightly.

6   Wrap the other end of the tape around the LED's shorter lead.

7   Watch the LED light up. Disconnect one of the tape ends to shut off the LED.

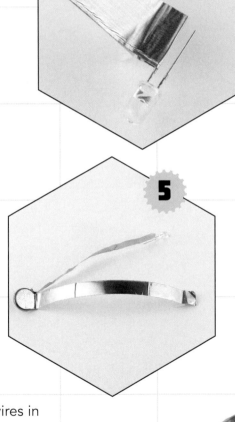

 FACT The copper tape works like the wires in your home or your electrical gadgets. The copper allows electrical current to flow from the battery to the LED. It then flows back in a loop.

FACT Most metals, including copper, are conductive, which mean they allow electricity to flow through them. Copper tape comes with conductive backing and non-conductive backing. The conductive backing means electricity will flow on both the top and bottom of the tape. Nonconductive backing will make your connections weaker and more unreliable.

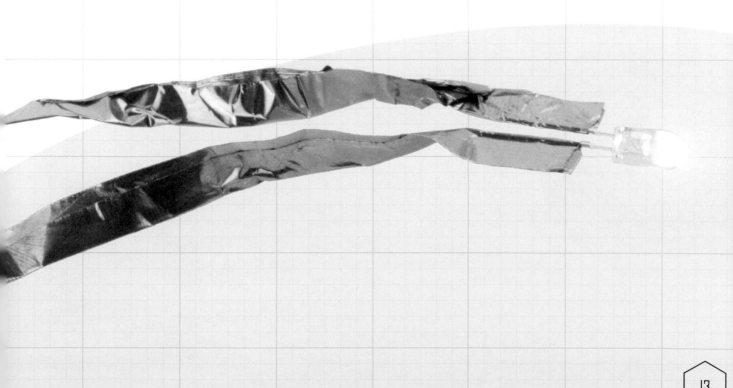

PARALLEL CIRCUITS

Sometimes a power source charges more than one light or gadget. One battery can light up many LEDs. Make a string of lights by building on what you've already learned.

YOU'LL NEED

> Simple Circuit

> 8.5-by-11-inch (21.5-by-28-cm) piece of paper

> two 5mm LEDs

STEPS

1 Set the Simple Circuit on your workspace. Carefully peel away the remaining backing on the copper strips.

2 Lay the circuit on the paper.

3 Slightly bend the leads on one of the LEDs.

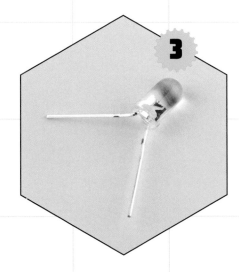

FACT The circuit you created is called a parallel circuit. Electricity passes through the LEDs at the same time. You can place many bulbs in this circuit. Each will receive the full current from the battery. Your house is wired as a parallel circuit. You can unplug some things while others still work. Also, equal current will flow to all your lights and gadgets.

4   Slide the LED's longer lead under the tape attached to the '+' side of the battery. Press down on the tape to hold it still.

5   Slide its shorter lead under the tape attached to the '-' lead. Press the tape down tightly.

6   Repeat steps 4 and 5 with another LED.

TRY THIS Remove one LED. The others will continue to glow.

SERIES CIRCUITS

A circuit made by connecting batteries and LEDs all in one loop is called a series circuit. A series circuit is different than a parallel circuit—can you figure out how?

YOU'LL NEED

> two CR2032 batteries

> three 6-inch- (15-cm-) long pieces of conductive copper tape

> two 5mm LEDs

STEPS

1   Stack the batteries with the '+' sides facing up.

2   Peel a ½-inch (1.3-cm) section of backing from each end of the copper tape pieces.

3   Stick one end of a piece or copper tape to the '+' side of the battery stack.

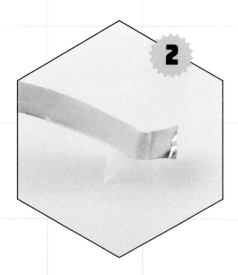

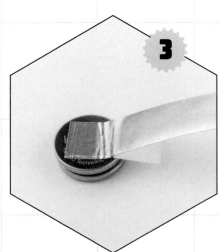

4   Wrap the other end of this piece of copper around a LED's longer lead.

5   Stick one end of another piece of tape to the '-' side of the battery stack. Make sure the pieces of copper angle away from one another.

6   Wrap the end of this piece of copper around the second LED's shorter lead.

FACT You need an extra battery to connect several LEDs in series. Why is that? As electricity flows through each bulb, it reduces the power from the battery. The bulbs will grow dimmer each time another is added.

7   Connect the loose leads with the remaining piece of copper.

8   Watch the LED light up. Disconnect any of the tape ends to shut off the LED.

FACT You have created a series circuit. The electricity's path flows from one LED to the next. Each bulb is part of the loop. Try adding more bulbs and copper to make the loop bigger. How many can you add to a pair of batteries before you run out of power?

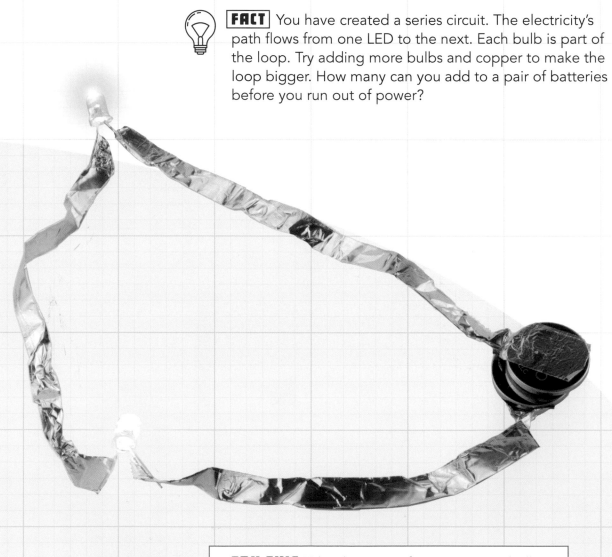

TRY THIS What happens if you remove a bulb? The other LEDs will not work because you have stopped the flow of electrical current. A parallel circuit has many loops for current to flow in. A series circuit is only a single loop.

LIGHT UP THE SKY

Watch where you're going! Fold a paper airplane that people will see coming from far away—even in the dark.

YOU'LL NEED

> 8.5-by-11-inch (21.5-by-28-cm) piece of paper

> ruler

> pencil

> scissors

> three CR2032 batteries

> clear tape

> two 1 ½-inch- (4-cm-) long pieces of conductive copper tape

> two white 5mm LEDs

> three 4-inch- (10-cm-) long pieces of conductive copper tape

> green 5mm LED

> red 5mm LED

STEPS

1 Fold the paper in half lengthwise. Unfold it.

2 Turn the paper vertically on your work surface. Fold the top two corners in, toward the crease.

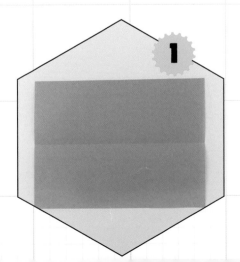

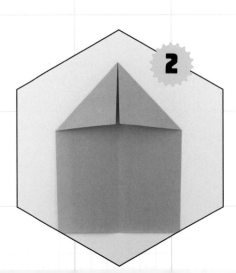

3　Fold the top corners in again, so the long sides of the triangles meet in the middle of the paper.

4　Fold the airplane in half.

5　Measure and mark a line 1 inch (2.5 cm) from the bottom of the creased edge.

6　Fold along the line you just made. This will make the plane's wings.

7　Cut a small notch on the bottom of the plane. It should be about 2 inches (5 cm) from the pointed nose.

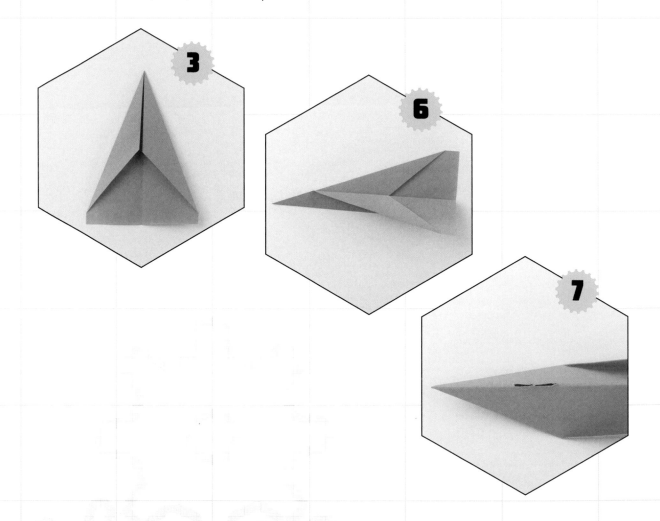

8   Set a battery on top of the notch. It should stick out about a ½ inch (1.3 cm) from the bottom of the plane. Make the notch larger, if necessary. Tape the battery in place.

9   Remove the backing on one of the 1 ½ inch (4 cm) pieces of tape. Attach one piece of tape to the side of the battery. Angle the tape toward the nose of the plane. Don't press down on the tape.

10 Repeat step 9 with the second piece of tape on the other side of the battery.

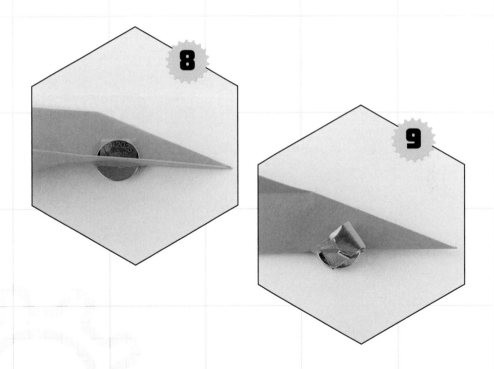

11　Stick the leads of the white LEDs under the copper tape. Make sure the longer leads are touching the copper tape attached to the '+' side of the battery. The lights should light up. Press the tape down.

12　Trim off any extra tape. Do not let the copper strips touch each other.

13　Cut a small notch on the bottom of the plane. It should be about 1 inch (2.5 cm) from the back.

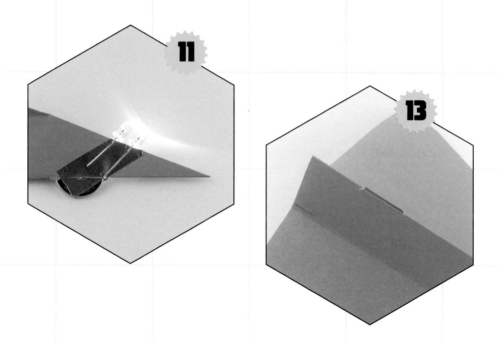

 FACT In this project you used both a parallel and a series circuit. Which circuit is in series? Which is in parallel?

TIP Stacking two batteries doubles their power!

14   Set two batteries on top of the notch. They should stick out about a ½ inch (1.3 cm) from the bottom of the plane. The '+' sides should face out. Tape the batteries in place.

15   Remove the backing on one of the longer pieces of copper tape. Attach one piece of tape to the '+' side of a battery. Run the tape up the sides of the plane and under the wings. Do not press down on the tape.

16   Place the leads of the green LED under the tape on the right wing. Press the tape down.

17   Repeat step 15 with the second piece of tape on the other side of the plane.

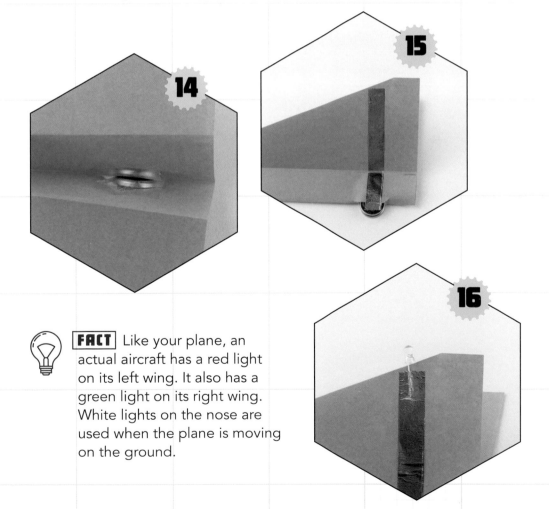

FACT Like your plane, an actual aircraft has a red light on its left wing. It also has a green light on its right wing. White lights on the nose are used when the plane is moving on the ground.

18. Place the leads of the red LED under the tape on the left wing. Press the tape down.

19. Remove the backing on the remaining piece of copper tape. Lay it across the top of the plane to connect the loose leads.

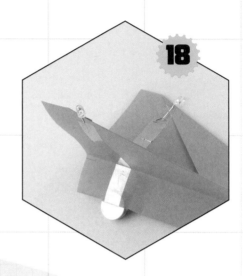

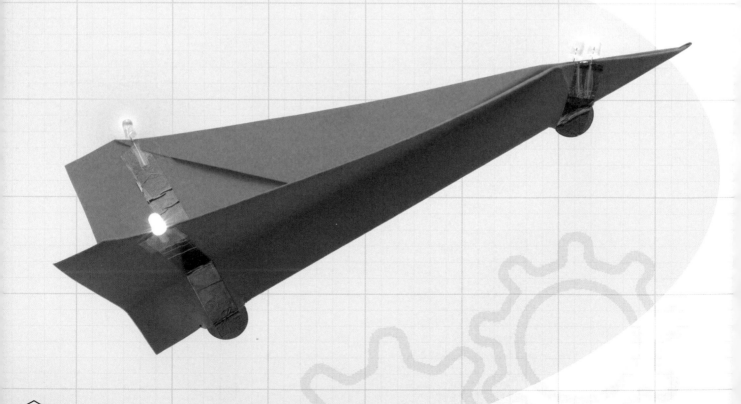

WORKING WITH BREADBOARDS

Most electronics use melted metal, called solder, to fuse pieces together. But you can also make circuits without soldering by using a breadboard. These plastic boards are full of holes. Insert wires or leads into the holes to test out circuits before joining them permanently.

BREADBOARD CIRCUITS AND SWITCHES

Test out your circuit-making skills by adding a switch! Does your light turn on and off when it's supposed to?

YOU'LL NEED

> half-sized breadboard

> 220 ohm resistor

> mini push button switch

> 5mm LED

> small jumper wire

> 9 volt battery

> 9 volt battery connector

STEPS

1 Start at row 10 on the left side of the breadboard. Push one leg of the resistor into the '+' (red) power strip.

2 Connect its other leg to the first hole in terminal strip 10.

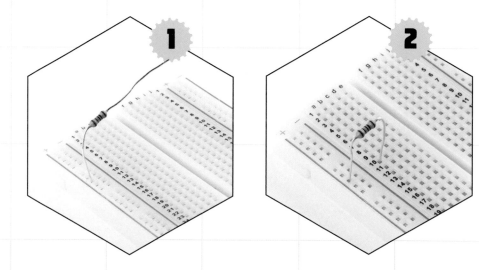

3 Push one leg of the push button switch in next hole in row 10.

4 Connect the other leg of the switch to a hole in row 11.

5 Push the '+' LED lead to the hole next to it in row 11.

6 Connect the '-' LED lead to a hole in row 11 across the center of the breadboard.

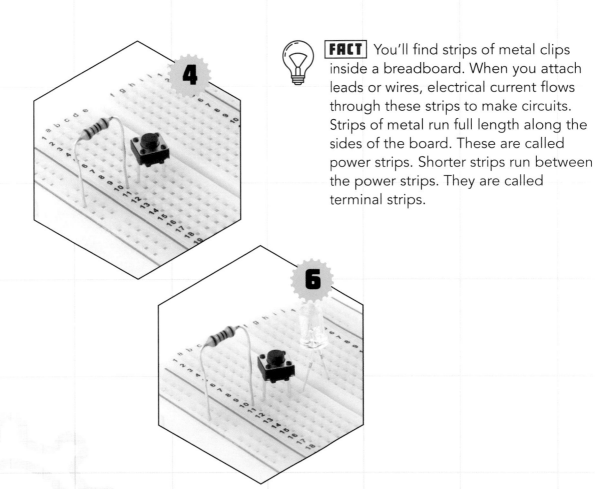

FACT You'll find strips of metal clips inside a breadboard. When you attach leads or wires, electrical current flows through these strips to make circuits. Strips of metal run full length along the sides of the board. These are called power strips. Shorter strips run between the power strips. They are called terminal strips.

 FACT The smaller terminal on a 9 volt battery is the '+' terminal.

7   Push one end of the jumper wire next to the '-' lead in row 11.

8   Connect its other end to the '-' power strip.

9   Attach the battery to the battery connector.

10 Plug the '-' wire on the connector to the '-' power strip on the right side of the breadboard.

11 Plug the '+' wire on the connecter to the '+' power strip on the left side of the breadboard.

12 Press the push button switch to light the LED.

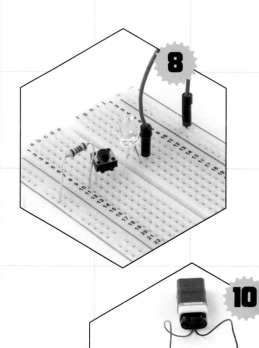

TRY THIS Your project makes a circuit that loops the battery's current around the board. There are many different ways to arrange how the leads connect to each other. Try making and testing your own! Just remember that there must be a continuous loop of metal. Where the strips are separated by plastic, no current will flow.

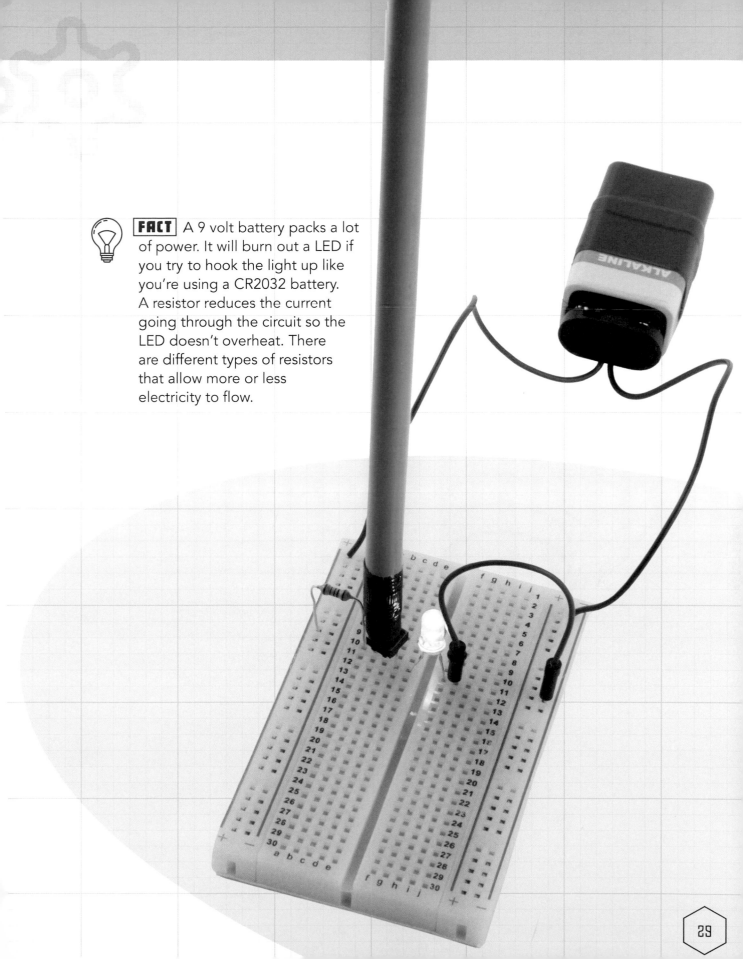

FACT A 9 volt battery packs a lot of power. It will burn out a LED if you try to hook the light up like you're using a CR2032 battery. A resistor reduces the current going through the circuit so the LED doesn't overheat. There are different types of resistors that allow more or less electricity to flow.

LEDs IN PARALLEL

You can create all kinds of circuits with a breadboard. Try this project to make a colorful parallel circuit.

YOU'LL NEED

- half-sized breadboard
- four 220 ohm resistors
- four 5mm LEDs
- four small jumper wires
- 9 volt battery
- 9 volt battery connector

STEPS

1 Start at row 10. Connect one leg of a resistor to the '+' (red) power strip.

2 Connect its other leg to the first hole in terminal strip 10.

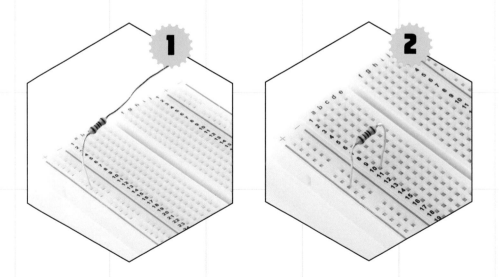

3 Put the '+' lead of an LED into another hole in row 10.

4 Put the '-' lead into a row 10 hole across the center of the breadboard.

5 Place one leg of a jumper wire next to the lead in row 10.

6 Connect the other end of the wire to the '-' power strip.

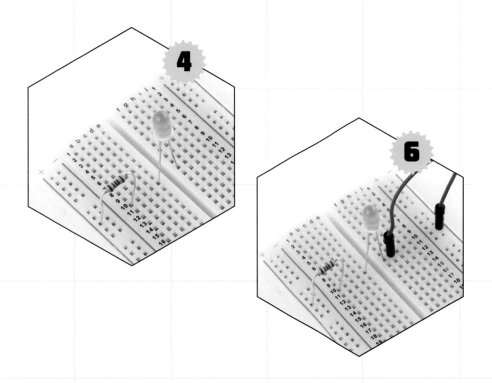

 FACT Each bulb in a parallel circuit receives the full current from the battery. This means that each LED must have its own resistor.

7   Repeat steps 1–6 at row 15.

8   Repeat steps 1–6 at row 20.

9   Repeat steps 1–6 at row 25.

10   Attach the battery to the battery connector.

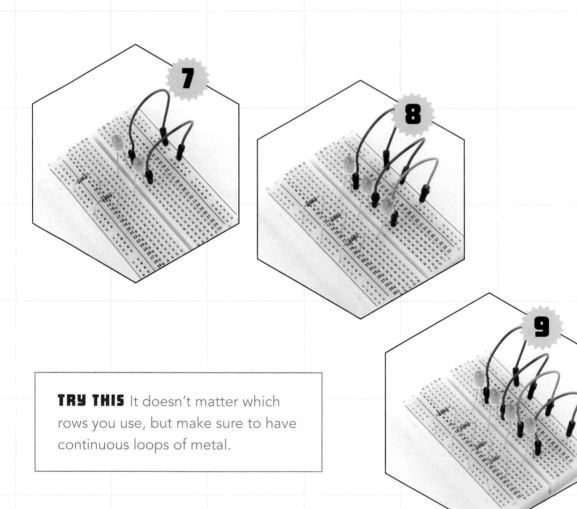

TRY THIS It doesn't matter which rows you use, but make sure to have continuous loops of metal.

11 Plug the '+' battery wire into the '+' power strip.

12 Plug the '-' battery wire into the '-' power strip. The LED should light up.

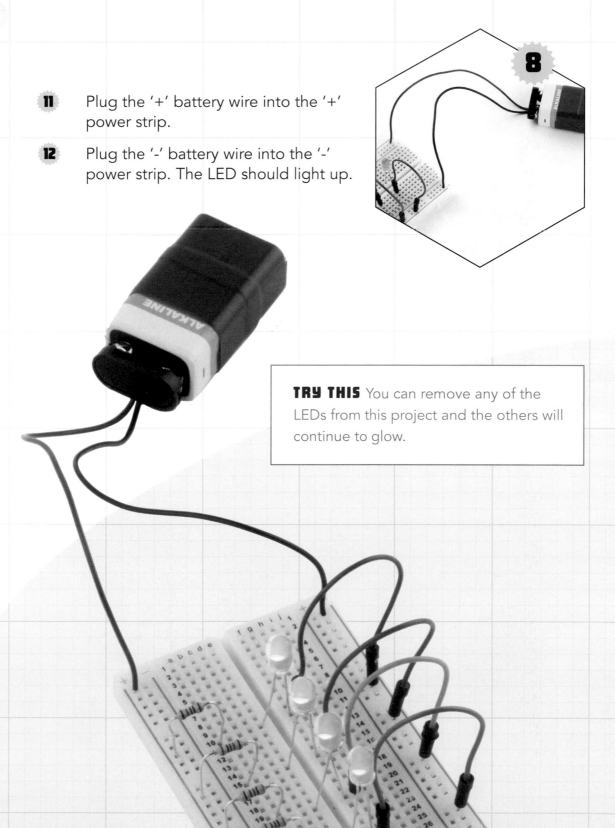

TRY THIS You can remove any of the LEDs from this project and the others will continue to glow.

LEDs IN SERIES

You can use a breadboard to make all the same types of circuits you can make with wire or solder. Try out making a series circuit with this project.

YOU'LL NEED

- half-sized breadboard
- 220 ohm resistor
- four 5mm LEDs

- small jumper wire
- 9 volt battery
- 9 volt battery connecter

STEPS

1 Start at row 10. Connect one leg of a resistor to the '+' (red) power strip.

2 Connect its other leg to the first hole in terminal strip 10.

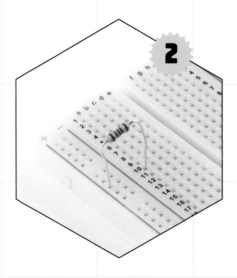

 FACT The resistor reduces electrical current for the whole loop. You need only one resistor for a series circuit. Why? The LEDs and resistor are all part of one loop.

3 Stick the '+' lead of an LED into another hole in row 10.

4 Connect the '-' lead to a hole in row 15.

5 Connect a '+' LED lead to another hole in row 15.

6 Stick the '-' lead into a hole in row 20.

7 Connect a '+' LED lead to another hole in row 20.

8 Stick the '-' lead into a hole in row 25, across the center of the breadboard.

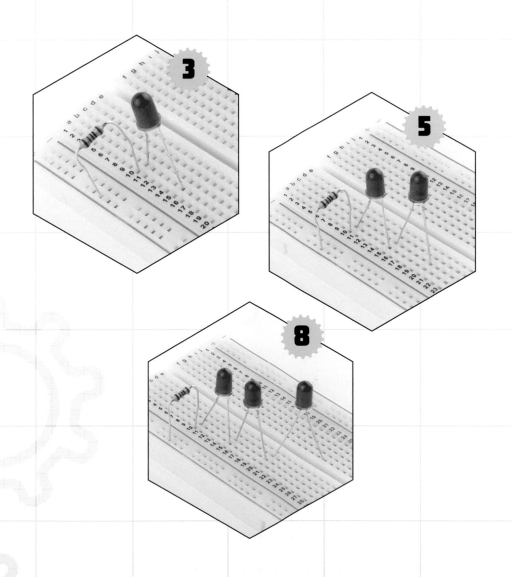

9 Connect one leg of the jumper wire near this lead in row 25.

10 Connect its other end to the '-' power strip.

11 Attach the battery to the battery connector.

12 Push the '+' battery wire into the '+' power strip.

13 Push the '-' battery wire into the '-' power strip.

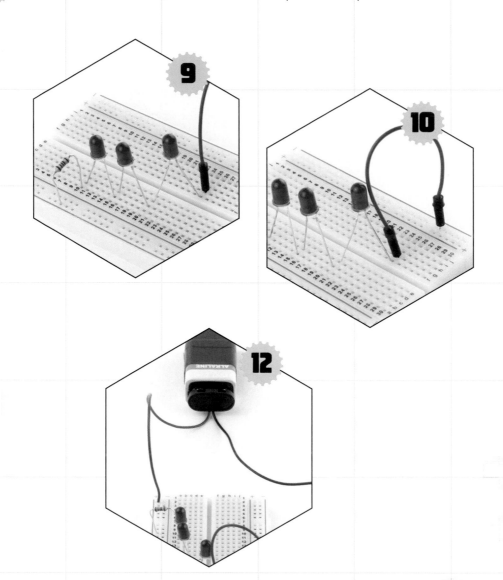

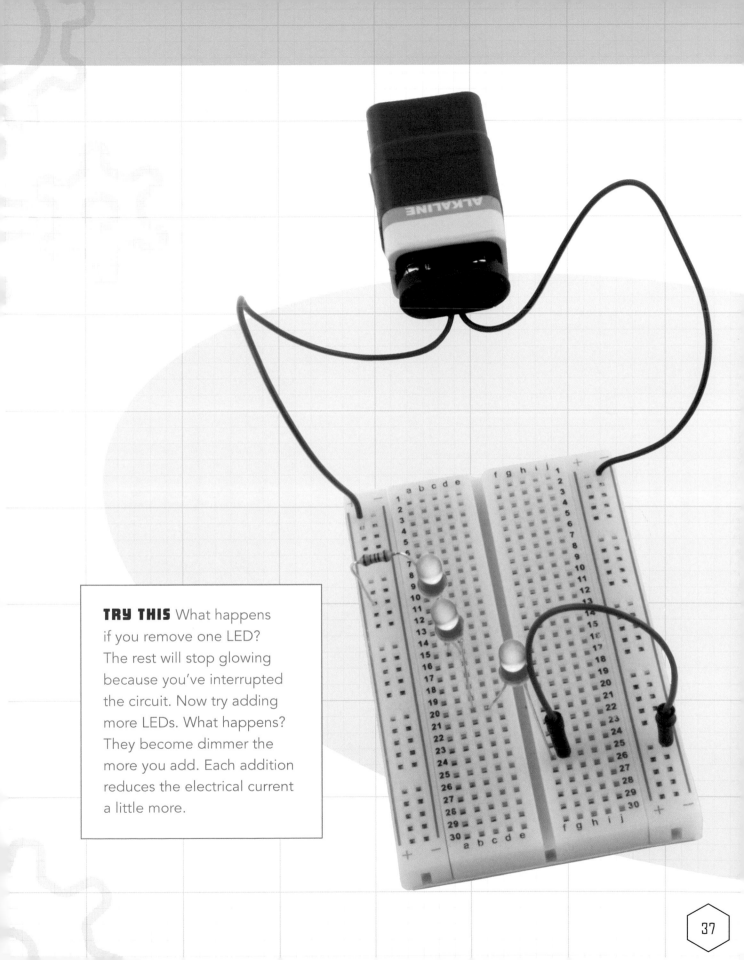

TRY THIS What happens if you remove one LED? The rest will stop glowing because you've interrupted the circuit. Now try adding more LEDs. What happens? They become dimmer the more you add. Each addition reduces the electrical current a little more.

USING A TILT SWITCH

A switch interrupts electrical current in a circuit when it is switched off. It allows current when switched on. You experimented with a simple switch on your breadboard. Take it to the next level by adding some movement!

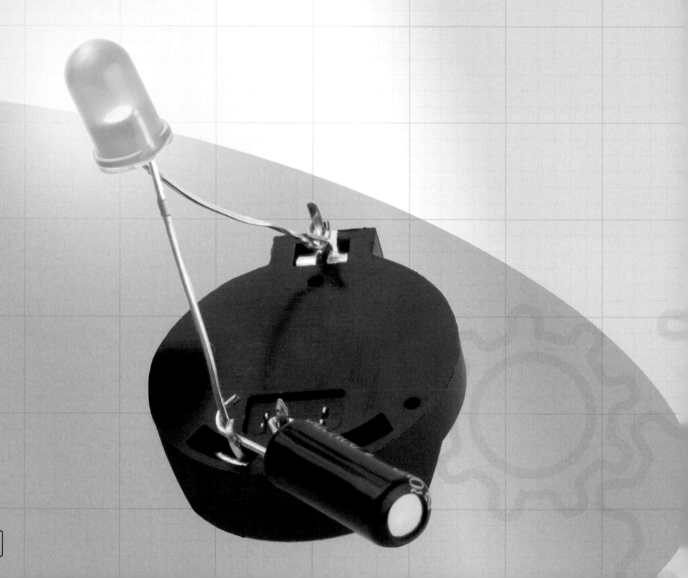

PROJECT 4, LEVEL 1
WIRED TILT SWITCH CIRCUIT

A tilt switch is a kind of switch that turns on and off when you tilt it. It can add a fun feature to your LED projects!

YOU'LL NEED

> CR2032 battery

> CR2032 battery holder

> 5mm LED

> small tilt switch

STEPS

1 Place the battery in the holder.

2 Carefully bend each of the LED leads into a tiny loop.

3 Place the loop on the longer lead around the connection on the '+' side of the battery. Make it as tight as possible.

4 Bend one of the leads on the tilt switch into a tiny loop.

5 Fit this loop around the '-' battery connection.

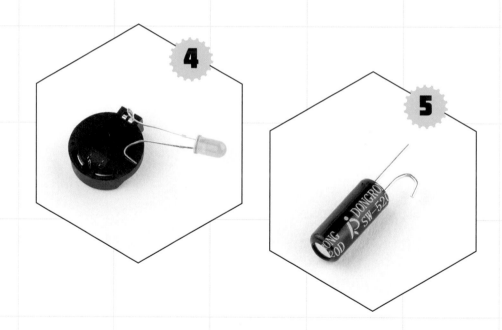

 FACT Like batteries, battery holders have '+' and '-' sides. Make sure the longer LED lead is attached to the '+' side. Don't let any of the wires touch. This could cause a short. A short happens when electricity follows an unplanned path.

6 Connect the other tilt switch lead to the loose LED lead.

7 Carefully tilt the project back and forth.

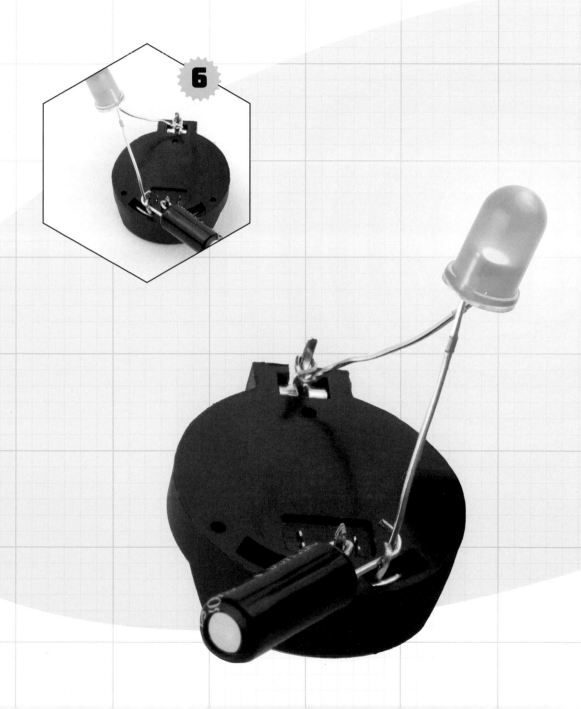

SOLDERED TILT SWITCH CIRCUIT

Your tilt switch project is fun. But it's hard to keep the wires tightly connected. It stops working if the wires become loose. Soldering the wires together will make the connections strong and permanent.

YOU'LL NEED

> Wired Tilt Switch Circuit

> piece of wood for a work surface

> low heat soldering iron

> solder

STEPS

1   Place the Wired Tilt Switch Circuit on the wood.

2   Hold the hot soldering iron tip on one side of one of the looped connections.

3 Hold a piece of soldering wire on the other side of the connection. Don't touch the solder to the tip of the iron.

4 When the wires heat up, the solder will flow onto the wires and connect them. Quickly remove the soldering iron tip as the solder begins to flow.

5 Blow on the connection to cool it. Do not touch it until it cools.

6 Repeat steps 3–7 to solder the other two connections.

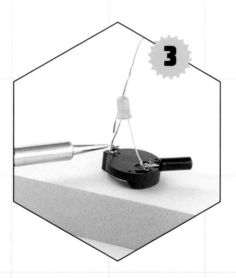

3

 FACT Do not get the soldering iron too close to the plastic battery holder. It will melt.

FACT For your safety, always wear eye protection when soldering. And never touch the tip of the soldering iron or hot solder.

TRY THIS Soldering will make your connections stronger. Get some practice by soldering copper tape projects. The flat tape will make it easier to work with when you're just starting out.

LIGHT SWORD

Want a sword that lights up as you swing it into action? Use your tilt switch project to power up this DIY LED project.

 YOU'LL NEED

- Soldered Tilt Switch project
- 8-inch- (20-cm-) long piece of 1-inch (2.5-cm) wide PVC
- hot glue and hot glue gun

- end cap for 1-inch (25-mm) PVC
- 9-inch- (23-cm-) long piece of plastic hose, 1 inch (2.5 cm) in diameter
- black paint (optional)

STEPS

1 Slide the Soldered Tilt Switch Circuit into the bottom end of the PVC.

2 Adjust the tilt switch so that the LED lights up when you tilt it upward.

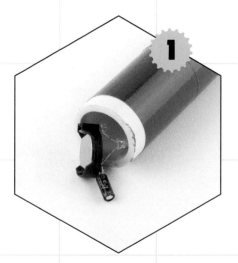
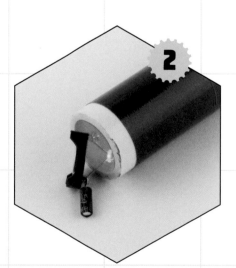

47

3 Glue the battery holder to the inside of the pipe. The battery should stick partway out of the pipe so you can change it when needed.

4 Slide on the end cap to cover the battery.

5 Insert the hose about 1 inch into the other end of the PVC. Glue it in place.

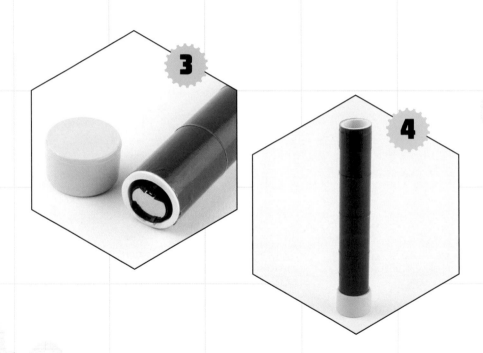

6 Paint the PVC handle.

7 As you swing the sword into action, it will light up.

🔆 **FACT** Make sure your sword is switched off when you're not using it.

TRY THIS Change the color of the LEDs you use.

READ MORE

Enz, Tammy. *Electronics Projects For Beginners.* Junior Makers 4D. North Mankato, Minn.: Capstone Press, 2018.

Leigh, Helen. *Crafty Kid's Guide to DIY Electronics: 20 Fun Projects for Makers, Crafters, and Everyone in Between.* New York: McGraw-Hill Education, 2018.

Murphy, Maggie. *High-Tech DIY Projects With Electronics, Sensors, and LEDs.* Maker Kids. New York: PowerKids Press, 2015.

INTERNET SITES

Use FactHound to find Internet sites related to this book.
Visit *www.facthound.com*
Just type in 9781543528466 and go.